Herr Kutter, The Barbaric Barber

or

The Villain Never Could Get His Part Right

A Melodrama in One Act

by Billy St. John

A SAMUEL FRENCH ACTING EDITION

New York Hollywood London Toronto
SAMUELFRENCH.COM

Copyright © 2006 by Billy St. John

ALL RIGHTS RESERVED

CAUTION: Professionals and amateurs are hereby warned that *HERR KUTTER, THE BARBARIC BARBER* is subject to a Licensing Fee. It is fully protected under the copyright laws of the United States of America, the British Commonwealth, including Canada, and all other countries of the Copyright Union. All rights, including professional, amateur, motion picture, recitation, lecturing, public reading, radio broadcasting, television and the rights of translation into foreign languages are strictly reserved. In its present form the play is dedicated to the reading public only.

The amateur live stage performance rights to *HERR KUTTER, THE BARBARIC BARBER* are controlled exclusively by Samuel French, Inc., and licensing arrangements and performance licenses must be secured well in advance of presentation. PLEASE NOTE that amateur Licensing Fees are set upon application in accordance with your producing circumstances. When applying for a licensing quotation and a performance license please give us the number of performances intended, dates of production, your seating capacity and admission fee. Licensing Fees are payable one week before the opening performance of the play to Samuel French, Inc., at 45 W. 25th Street, New York, NY 10010.

Licensing Fee of the required amount must be paid whether the play is presented for charity or gain and whether or not admission is charged.

Stock licensing fees quoted upon application to Samuel French, Inc.

For all other rights than those stipulated above, apply to: Samuel French, Inc.

Particular emphasis is laid on the question of amateur or professional readings, permission and terms for which must be secured in writing from Samuel French, Inc.

Copying from this book in whole or in part is strictly forbidden by law, and the right of performance is not transferable.

Whenever the play is produced the following notice must appear on all programs, printing and advertising for the play: "Produced by special arrangement with Samuel French, Inc."

Due authorship credit must be given on all programs, printing and advertising for the play.

ISBN 978-0-573-63261-7   Printed in U.S.A.   #9983

No one shall commit or authorize any act or omission by which the copyright of, or the right to copyright, this play may be impaired.

No one shall make any changes in this play for the purpose of production.

Publication of this play does not imply availability for performance. Both amateurs and professionals considering a production are strongly advised in their own interests to apply to Samuel French, Inc., for written permission before starting rehearsals, advertising, or booking a theatre.

No part of this book may be reproduced, stored in a retrieval system, or transmitted in any form, by any means, now known or yet to be invented, including mechanical, electronic, photocopying, recording, videotaping, or otherwise, without the prior written permission of the publisher.

IMPORTANT BILLING AND CREDIT REQUIREMENTS

All producers of **HERR KUTTER, THE BARBARIC BARBER** must give credit to the Author of the Play in all programs distributed in connection with performances of the Play, and in all instances in which the title of the Play appears for the purposes of advertising, publicizing or otherwise exploiting the Play and/or a production. The name of the Author must appear on a separate line on which no other name appears, immediately following the title and must appear in size of type not less than fifty percent of the size of the title type.

CAST OF CHARACTERS

PAT — The play's stage manager. Male. 20's or older. Tense.

STAGEHAND — Male. (Non-speaking role.) 20's or older. Stage shy.

HERR HANS KUTTER — 30's, the villain. A barber. German.

HEDDA WOOD — 20's or 30's, the villainess, Hans' manicurist. Has a Brooklyn accent.

KITTY LITTER — 40's, wealthy, owns a string of coiffure salons.

LORRIE ELL — 20's, her niece, pretty, the heroine.

NELL POLISH — 20's, Kitty's manicurist, cute and bubbly.

MINNIE BUCKS — 40's or older, wealthy, a bank president's wife.

LOTTA SCRIBBLES — 40's or older, a newspaper society columnist.

BOO (BETTY LOU) FOUNT — 20's, Kitty's stylist, girlish.

BEA HIVE — 30's, Kitty's stylist, mature demeanor, pleasant.

OFFICER DAN DRUFF — 20's or older, a policeman, Nell's boyfriend.

HARRY NOGGIN — 20's, boyish, a barber, the hero.

BARBARA POLE — 20's, Harry's manicurist, good-natured.

SHU (SHUBERT) SHINER — 20's, Harry's shoeshine man, likes to joke.

EXTRAS (if desired) — Hair Ball guests.

SYNOPSIS OF SCENES

Prologue	The forestage.
Scene 1	Hans' Barber Shop. A Monday.
Scene 2	Kitty's home. Shortly after.
Scene 3	Miss Kitty's Coiffure Salon. Later that morning.
Scene 4	Harry's Barber Shop. That morning.
Scene 5	Hans' Barber Shop. Shortly after.
Scene 6	Harry's Barber Shop. Later that morning.
Scene 7	Kitty's home. That afternoon.
Scene 8	Various New York locations. Saturday night.
Scene 9	The Hair Ball. Shortly after.
Scene 10	The veranda. Immediately following.
Scene 11	The Hair Ball. Immediately following.

TIME
1900

PLACE
New York City

Prologue

(The house lights dim out. A STAGEHAND ENTERS DL, in the dark, and sets a full length mirror on a stand DL in front of the main curtain. As he does this, PAT, the STAGE MANAGER, sticks his head in DR.)

PAT. *(In the darkness. He calls the light board operator by his/her real first name, talking in a loud whisper.)*, can you turn up the lights down right? *(An area light comes up DL on the STAGEHAND putting the mirror in place. STAGEHAND freezes, looking as startled as a deer in headlights.)* Down RIGHT! *(The light DL fades out as an area light DR fades up. STAGEHAND EXITS DL. PAT's head is sticking out DR. To the audience.)* Uh...hi. .sorry to do this but... um... *(He steps out all the way. He carries a clip board.)* I'm Pat. I'm the stage manager for this show. Look, I know it's really unusual for a stage manager to talk to the audience before the show, but I'm in charge of the play once the curtain opens, and there are a few things I feel I have to tell you. For one thing, some of the actors don't get along very well...

LORRIE. *(Off DL.)* There's a reason for that.

PAT. *(Glaring off DL; a warning.)* ...but I trust that won't affect their performances! *(Turning back to the audience.)* Also, if you looked in your program, you saw that *(Gives the actor's real name.)* plays the villainous German barber, Herr Kutter. Well, *(Actor's real first name.)* had a little trouble learning his lines, and...uh...we never

HERR KUTTER, THE BARBARIC BARBER

got throught a single rehearsal without his making some mistakes. I'll be following in the script offstage, and if our villain's trolley jumps the tracks, so to speak, I'll do what I can to get the play back in line. Uh...well...I guess we should begin, so settle back and... *(He is interrupted as HANS' hand reaches in from off DR. He grabs PAT's arm and pulls him offstage.)*

HANS. *(Off DR.)* Why did you tell the audience I didn't learn my lines!?! I know my lines...I just get a little mixed up where to say them sometimes. It could happen to any of us.

ALL THE OTHER ACTORS. *(Offstage.)* Not me!

PAT. *(Off DR.)* Let go of my shirt!

(There is the sound of cloth ripping off DR.)

HANS. *(Off DR.)* Ooooops...

PAT. *(Off DR.)* You'll pay for that! Kill the area light! *(The light DR fades out. The curtain opens just enough to make a narrow gap. An angry hiss.)* Places!

HANS. *(Off DR.)* All right, I'm going. Where's *(says the real first name of the actress playing HEDDA.)*?

HEDDA. *(Off DR.)* I'm the one whose foot you're standing on, you big oaf! Come on!

(HANS and HEDDA ENTER in the dark and take their places DC at the curtain gap.)

PAT. *(Off DR. Exasperated.)* Lights...

HERR KUTTER, THE BARBARIC BARBER

Scene 1
Hans' Barber Shop. A Monday.

(An area light comes up DC on HANS and HEDDA. HANS, 30's, is, as we've heard, a villainous barber. He wears a dark suit and a pastel or pin striped shirt with white collar and cuffs. He has black hair parted in the middle and plastered to his head, and a pencil thin black moustache. He speaks with a German accent. HEDDA, 20's or 30's, is a typical vamp with heavy eye shadow, and bright red lips. She wears a black dress circa 1900. HANS holds one end of a razor strap, HEDDA the other. He strops a straight razor back and forth across it.)

HANS. *(To the audience.)* Good evening. I am Hans Kutter, a barber — duh best barber in New York. You could say I stand head und shoulders above duh rest. I haf a plan dat vill make me duh richest barber in New York as vell. I vas born in Germany, if you can't tell by my accent. You can call me Herr *(pronounced "hair")* Kutter. To achieve my goal, I vill haf to commit a little murder or two vich makes me duh villain of duh piece, I suppose.

HEDDA. *(With a strong Brooklyn accent.)* Murder? That's... that's barbaric!

HANS. Vhere do you tink duh title comes from?

HEDDA. Okay, I get it. Geeze, Hans, ain't cha gonna introduce me too?

HANS. Very vell. Dis iss my partner in crime, Hedda Vood.

HEDDA. Wood! Wood! Are you ever gonna learn to pronounce my name right? Hedda Wood!

HANS. Don't get your ka-knickers in a twist! I'm doing duh best I can! *(To the audience; sotto voice.)* Between you und me, Hedda's not duh sharpest pair of scissors in duh drawer. *(Out loud.)* Anyvay, dere iss dis udder barber named Harry Noggin who...

HERR KUTTER, THE BARBARIC BARBER

PAT. *(Off DR.)* Not yet!

HANS. *(To the audience.)* I'm getting ahead of myself.

HEDDA. You're gonna have an artist sculpt your head?

HANS. See vhat I mean? Vhat can I say? She vorks cheap.

HEDDA. Hey! Who you calling cheap!?!

HANS. If duh clodhopper fits...

PAT. *(STEPS IN from off DR. There is now a rip in his right shirt sleeve.)* Tell them about your plan! *(He STEPS OFF DR.)*

HANS. *(Mutters.)* Oh...yeah... *(Out loud.)* As I vas saying, I plan to become duh richest barber in New York. To do so, I must do avay vid von of duh vealthiest vomen in duh city, Miss Kitty Litter, cat lover and owner of numerous Miss Kitty's Coiffure Salons throughout Manhattan. Her fatal accident vill take place soon after I marry Miss Kitty's niece and heir, Miss Lorrie Ell, a very attractive young lady.

HEDDA. *(To the audience.)* That's a matter of opinion.

HANS. *(Irritated at HEDDA.)* As I vas saying...

PAT. *(Off DR.)* That's it! Stop!

HANS. *(To the audience, after shooting PAT a look offstage.)* You'll see vhat happens... *(The area light fades out. HANS and HEDDA EXIT off DR. To PAT, we presume.)* Was that good enough for you!?!

(The actor will not use the German accent when he's playing himself, nor will HEDDA use a Brooklyn accent when the actress is playing herself.)

HERR KUTTER, THE BARBARIC BARBER

Scene 2
Kitty's home. Shortly after.

(KITTY LITTER ENTERS DL and stands before the mirror. She is carrying the hat to her ensemble; it has a wide brim and a net sash that ties under the chin. After a beat, an area light DL comes up. KITTY is in her 40's, an attractive and well groomed woman. She wears a chic ensemble of the period, a long dress with mutton sleeves, and a full length coat. She checks herself in the mirror.)

LORRIE. *(Off DL.)* Aunt Kitty...?

KITTY. Come in, Lorrie, dear. *(LORRIE ELL ENTERS DL and comes to SR of KITTY. LORRIE is a pretty girl in her early 20's. She has long hair that cascades down her back. She wears wears a blouse with mutton sleeves and a long skirt of the period.)* I'm just checking my new outfit. What do you think?

LORRIE. It's beautiful, Aunt Kitty. Golly, I hope I look as good as you do when I'm over forty!

HEDDA. *(Off DR.)* Fat chance!

PAT. *(Off DR.)* Shuuu...

LORRIE. *(To KITTY, after shooting HEDDA a look.)* Your chauffeur, Wheeler, has brought the horseless carriage around, so whenever you're ready to go...

KITTY. Buying an automobile was extravagant, I know, but they're so stylish I couldn't resist. I'll need my hat, of course. A lady must protect her hair when zipping along at five miles an hour. Be glad you're still young enough to wear your tresses long and flowing.

HEDDA. *(Off DR.)* Ha! From behind, she looks like a horse's backside!

LORRIE. *(Turning to look at her offstage.)* You look like a

HERR KUTTER, THE BARBARIC BARBER

horse's backside from the front!
　　HEDDA. *(STEPS IN DR.)* Why you...

(PAT's arms reach in. He puts an arm around HEDDA's waist and his other hand over her mouth and pulls her off DR.)

　　KITTY. Speaking of hair, what do you think? *(She pats her hair.)*
　　LORRIE. Your hair is lovely, Aunt Kitty, and that style becomes you.
　　KITTY. Thank you, dear. *(She puts on the hat, tying it under her chin.)* I'm fortunate to employ the best beauticians in the New York to keep it impecably styled. I have to admit I'm very concerned about my looks.
　　HEDDA. *(Off DR.)* In that case, you'd better hire a plastic surgeon too...and soon! *(KITTY shoots a look off DR.)*
　　LORRIE. You are not only very attractive, you are truly an outstanding businesswoman, Auntie. You set an example for young women everywhere.
　　KITTY. By the time I reached thirty, being a wealthy debutant with no purpose in life had become boring, so I felt I needed a project to keep me occupied. That's when I opened my first salon. It was amazingly successful, so I opened another, then another, and before I knew it, I had salons all over the city.
　　HANS. *(STEPPING IN DR.)* Do you really think they need to hear all that?
　　KITTY. *(Through clenched teeth.)* Apparently, the playwright does!
　　HANS. What does he know? I think...

(He is interrupted as PAT's hand reaches out, grabs him, and PULLS HIM OFFSTAGE.)

HERR KUTTER, THE BARBARIC BARBER

KITTY. Speaking of the salons, I plan to hand deliver the invitations to my gala to my employees and the other local beauticians this morning. If you will, I'll have you deliver them to the barbers in Manhattan.

LORRIE. I'll be happy to, Aunt Kitty. They look beautiful. *(Quoting the invitation.)* "You are cordially invited to attend Miss Kitty Litter's Hair Ball."

KITTY. We'll mail them to the barbers and beauticians whose shops are outside the borough.

LORRIE. I hope the barbers you invite will attend, as well as the beauticians.

KITTY. There's no reason why they shouldn't — it's to raise money for a good cause: Kitty Litter's Shelter for Homeless Cats. Let's be on our way...as soon as I say goodbye to my little kitties.

LORRIE. All twenty-seven of them.

KITTY. Yes, and I love them, each and every one. Come, Lorrie, dear.

(They EXIT DL. The light fades down dim. STAGEHAND's arm sticks out DL. He moves it up and down, palm parallel to the floor, a signal to the light board operator to lower the lights all the way. The light fades out. We hear STAGEHAND ENTER, take the mirror, and EXIT DL. After a beat, we hear a crash and glass breaking.)

LORRIE. *(Off DL in the darkness.)* Bad luck...
PAT. *(Off DR in the darkness, an exasperated cry.)* Argggg... Curtain! Lights!

(The curtain opens and the lights come up SR on the main stage.)

HERR KUTTER, THE BARBARIC BARBER

Scene 3
Miss Kitty's Coiffure Salon. Later that morning.

(The set is divided into two sections: stage right is a Miss Kitty's Coiffure Salon, stage left is Harry Noggin's Barber Shop. Both are enclosed in a basic box set painted a light shade. [The walls will double as a ballroom later.] DR is the front door to the salon which opens out. UC is a pair of doorways with a narrow flat between them. A floral curtain on a rod covers the doorway SR; it leads to the salon's storeroom. A plain curtain on a rod covers the doorway SL; it leads to the barber shop's storeroom. Both curtains are backed with silvery cloth; they will be reversed for the ballroom set. DL is the barber shop's front door which opens out.

The two shops' furniture are parallel to and mirror each other. The salon, SR, has a folding screen made from narrow, hinged flats; it hides the UR corner of the salon. It is painted or covered with cloth that is feminine in style. A similar screen hides the UL corner of the barber shop. It is painted or covered with cloth that is masculine in style. The reverse sides of both screens are covered with glittery cloth; they will be reversed and moved in front of the furniture in both shops for the ballroom scene. A rectangular cabinet with two old-fashioned water pitchers and bowls stands in front of the screen SR; a similar cabinet with one pitcher and bowl stands in front of the screen SL. There are scissors, combs, hand mirrors and such on both cabinets. Two chairs for customers are in front of the cabinet SR; one chair is in front of the cabinet SL. Barber chairs would be ideal for all three, but ice cream chairs can be used in the salon and a simple wooden chair can be used in the barber shop. A small table and stool for the salon manicurist sit SRof the SR doorway UC when not in use. On the table are implements for nail care and a bowl

HERR KUTTER, THE BARBARIC BARBER

for tips.

AT RISE: On stage are beauticians BEA HIVE, 30's, behind the US chair, and BOO FAUNT, 20's, behind the DS chair. BEA has a mature demeanor and is pleasant. BOO is girlish. They wear long dresses of period. BEA's customer, LOTTA SCRIBBLES, 40's or older, sits on her chair US; she is a newspaper society columnist. BOO's customer, MINNIE BUCKS, 40's or older, sits on her chair DS; she is a wealthy banker's wife. Both wear the latest dresses of the period. Both wear their hair up in Gibson girl or similar styles. BEA and BOO are pinning their customers' hair in place. The manicurist, NELL POLISH, has her table and stool SR of MINNIE, and has just painted MINNIE's nails with clear polish. NELL, 20's, cute and bubbly, wears a skirt and blouse.)

BOO. All finished, Mrs. Bucks. The latest style from Paris. *(Hands her a hand mirror from the cabinet.)* It really becomes you.

MINNIE. *(Looking at herself.)* Oh, my... Is that really me?

BOO. *(Joking.)* Unless I accidently styled someone else's hair by mistake.

LOTTA. It's certainly a change from the bun you always wore. It looks wonderful, Minnie.

MINNIE. I think so, too. You did a lovely job, Miss Faunt.

BOO. Thank you. My name's Betty Lou, but call me Boo — everyone does.

MINNIE. *(Returning the mirror.)* Well, I couldn't be happier, Boo.

BEA. What about you, Mrs. Scribbles? *(Hands her a mirror.)* How do you like your new style?

LOTTA. *(Looking at herself.)* It's perfection, Bea.

NELL. You both look like you're ready to pose for that famous artist, Charles Dana Gibson.

HERR KUTTER, THE BARBARIC BARBER

LOTTA. Us? Gibson girls? Did you hear that, Minnie?
MINNIE. I hope my husband, Holder, thinks I look like a model.
LOTTA. I bet he will.
NELL. All finished.
LOTTA. *(Rising.)* Let's pay Bea and Boo; then we're going to pay a visit to your husband's bank.
MINNIE. *(Rising.)* Holder's bank? Why are we going there?
LOTTA. Because I want to see the look on his face when he sees the new you. If he faints, I hope it's onto a pile of nice, soft money.

(MINNIE laughs.)

BEA. Your purses, ladies.

(She and BOO take purses from the cabinet and give them to MINNIE and LOTTA who will take coins from them and pay BEA and BOO. They each put a coin into NELL's bowl on her table. KITTY ENTERS SR, carrying several invitations.)

KITTY. Good morning, girls. Minnie, Lotta, how nice to see you.

(LOTTA and MINNIE join her. They all do air kisses at the cheek.)

MINNIE. Good morning, Kitty.
LOTTA. Kitty...
KITTY. How fortuitous to see you here, Lotta. I was planning to drop by your office at the newspaper while I make my rounds.
LOTTA. Oh?
KITTY. I brought the invitations to a gala I'm hosting Saturday for the city's beauticians and barbers. These are for you, girls. *(BEA*

HERR KUTTER, THE BARBARIC BARBER

and BOO cross to SR of her. She gives them and NELL invitations. To LOTTA.) Here's the one I was going to bring you later, Lotta. *(Gives her one.)* I hope you can attend, as well, and mention us in your society column. *(LOTTA reads it as MINNIE looks over her shoulder. The others read theirs as well.)*

HANS. *(ENTERING DR. To the audience.)* You want me to wake you when this scene's over? *(The women glare at him. PAT's hand reaches in and pulls HANS OFFSTAGE.)* If you don't stop doing that, my right arm is going to be two inches longer than my left one!

LOTTA. *(Reading.)* "Kitty Litter's Hair Ball." I wouldn't miss it! And I shall certainly write about it in my column.

MINNIE. *(Pouting.)* I wish I could attend, but if it's just for barbers and beauticians...*(A look at LOTTA.)*...and society columnists...

KITTY. You and Holder come too, Minnie. Afterward, you can help spread the word about my new charity, a shelter for homeless cats. That's why I'm having the gala — to raise money for them.

(All the women begin to chatter, ad-libbing about the ball as the lights SR fade out. They EXIT. All but KITTY change into their ball gowns.)

HERR KUTTER, THE BARBARIC BARBER

Scene 4
Harry's Barber Shop. That morning.

(The lights fade up SL. HARRY NOGGIN ENTERS UC. He is an attractive young man in his 20's, a barber. He wears dark slacks and a pastel or striped shirt with white collar and cuffs.)

HARRY. What a lovely day!

HANS. *(ENTERING DR.)* Hold it! Wait a minute! *(HARRY stops and looks at HANS.)*

PAT. *(Off DR.)* What's he doing?

HEDDA. *(Off DR.)* I have no idea.

HANS. I don't mean to interrupt...well, I guess I do 'cause I just did...anyway, I know the playwright has to introduce all the characters in the show, including Harry Noggin, the hero, over there, but I think he made a big mistake by not bringing Herr Kutter back in sooner. I mean, I am playing the title role, right?

HARRY. Good grief!

HANS. I don't mean to upset you, *(Calls the actor by his real first name)*, but you know it's true. The title isn't "Harry Noggin, the Boyish Barber", is it?

HARRY. No, but the writer didn't title it "*(Calls the actor playing HANS' whole name)*, the Half-Baked Ham" either, did he?

HANS. *(Confidentially, to the audience.)* Male Juvenile Leads can be so touchy.

PAT. *(Off DR.) (Calls HANS' real first name)*, get back here!

HANS. So can stage managers. As I was saying... *(PAT's hand reaches out from off DR. He grabs HANS arm and pulls him offstage.)* Ow! There's an arm in that sleeve, you know!

PAT. *(Off DR.)* Hush! *(Calls the actor playing HARRY's real first name)*, make your entrance again. *(HARRY EXITS UC.)* Lights down.

HERR KUTTER, THE BARBARIC BARBER

(The light SL fades out.)

HEDDA. *(Off DR.)* I don't know why you're acting so snippy — at least you're getting to play the part you wanted.

HANS. *(Off DR.)* Who did you want to play?

HEDDA. *(Off DR.)* The heroine, Lorrie Ell, of course...or if not her, then Kitty Litter. But who do I have to be? Dumb old Hedda Wood. I just detest *(Says the actress who plays Lorrie's whole name)* and *(the actress who plays Kitty's whole name)* for getting parts that I should have been considered for!

HANS. *(Off DR.)* For what it's worth, they can't stand you, either.

PAT. *(Off DR.)* Will you two stuff a sock in it! Lights up! *(The lights SL fade up. HARRY ENTERS UC.)*

HARRY. *(Mutters to himself.)* It's about time. *(Out loud.)* What a lovely day! And how lucky am I, Harry Noggin, to own my own little barber shop where I can toil and earn an honest living. All I need now to make my life complete is the love of a good woman — a wife. If only the Fates would decree that I would meet her soon!

(LORRIE ENTERS SL, carrying an envelope.)

LORRIE. Hello. I...

(She catches her breath and puts a hand to her heart. HARRY does likewise. STAGEHAND's hands are thrust into view DL. He holds a triangle and metal wand. He makes twinkling notes on the triangle, signifying love has occurred.)

HANS. *(Off SR.)* Give me a break! *(STAGEHAND's arms withdraw.)*

HERR KUTTER, THE BARBARIC BARBER

LORRIE. *(To herself.)* Oh! What an attractive young man! The sight of him has brought a lump to my throat!

HANS. *(Off DR.)* It makes me want to throw up, too. *(HARRY shoots him a look DR.)*

HARRY. *(Back in character; to himself.)* Oh! What a lovely young woman! The very sight of her lights a fire within me!

HEDDA. *(Off DR.)* Indigestion.

LORRIE. *(To off DR.)* Shut up!

HARRY. May I help you, Miss...?

LORRIE. Ell — Lorrie Ell.

HARRY. I am Harry Noggin. It's a pleasure to meet you.

(He extends his hand. They shake. STAGEHAND does the triangle bit again DL, this time beating it even louder than before.)

HANS. *(ENTERING DR with his hands over his ears. To the audience.)* I don't know if I can go on — I've got this terrible ringing in my ears.

(PAT's hand reaches out, grabs HANS, and pulls him offstage.)

LORRIE. It is a pleasure to meet you as well; I believe you are the person I hoped to see. Are you not the barber who owns this establishment?

HARRY. I am.

LORRIE. *(Giving him the envelope.)* This is for you. It is an invitation to my aunt Kitty Litter's Hair Ball.

HARRY. The owner of the Miss Kitty's Coiffure Salons is your aunt?

LORRIE. Indeed, she is. Aunt Kitty wants to gather all of the beauticians and barbers in New York together to request their help — your help — in raising money for homeless cats.

HERR KUTTER, THE BARBARIC BARBER

HARRY. How can we be of service?

LORRIE. I'm glad you asked.

HANS. *(Off DR.)* I'll bet you are — it's not easy to get all this exposition out of the way.

LORRIE. At the dance, she is going to request that all of you place collection boxes in your businesses where your customers can, hopefully, donate to Aunt Kitty's worthwhile cause.

HARRY. Her concern for unfortunate felines is commendable. Will you be at the ball, Miss Ell?

LORRIE. Yes. I shall.

HARRY. Then I shall gladly attend.

LORRIE. How wonderful! I mean, I look forward to seeing you there.

HARRY. And I, you.

LORRIE. Well, then... Until Saturday.

HARRY. Saturday... *(They look lovingly into each other's eyes.)*

HANS. *(ENTERING DR.)* They get the idea! Move it along so we can get to my next scene!

(HARRY and LORRIE shoot daggers at him. He holds his hands up, palms out, in an appologetic gesture and BACKS OFF DR.)

LORRIE. *(To HARRY.)* Goodbye.

HARRY. Goodbye. *(She EXITS SL. Dreamily.)* Can my prayers have been answered so quickly?

(The lights fade out. HARRY EXITS. In the dark, STAGEHAND takes HARRY's chair and moves it to DC as PAT takes the manicure table and stool from SR and moves it to SR of the chair now DC. During this, the curtain closes partially, leaving a gap for the chair and table. An area light fades up DC. STAGEHAND freezes.)

HERR KUTTER, THE BARBARIC BARBER

PAT. *(A hiss.)* Not yet!

(The light fades out. PAT and STAGEHAND EXIT. HANS crosses to US of the chair; he has removed his suit coat and wears a smock. HEDDA goes to the stool and sits; she wears a smock over her dress. DAN DRUFF ENTERS and sits in the chair. He covers his upper half with a barber cape, including his head. HANS holds an old-fashioned cup of shaving lather and a lather brush. A towel is draped over one shoulder.)

PAT. *(Off SR.)* NOW bring up the lights!

(The area light DC comes back up.)

Scene 5
Hans' Barber Shop. Shortly after.

HEDDA. *(Screams.)* You've cut off his head!

(DAN pulls the cape down off his head to his neck, then gives HEDDA his right hand to buff his nails. DAN, 20's, is a customer, dressed in dark slacks to a policeman's uniform, and a suitable shirt. He has a big [fake] handlebar moustache.)

DAN. I'm fine, Miss Wood. You know, my captain down at the police station tells me I've got a good head on my shoulders. I in-

HERR KUTTER, THE BARBARIC BARBER

tend to keep it there.

HEDDA. *(Giggles.)* You're such a kidder, Officer Druff.

HANS. I've finished with your hair. Are you ready for your shave, Dan?

DAN. I'm ready, Herr Kutter.

(HANS lathers his face. HEDDA buffs his nails. As the dialog continues, HANS moves DS of DAN, blocking DAN's face from the audience so they don't see HANS peel off half of DAN's moustache and hide it up one of his sleeves before covering DAN's lip with lather. Once DAN's beard area is covered with lather, HANS will move back US of DAN and set the cup and brush on HEDDA's table.)

HEDDA. When I'm through wid ja, your nails will look nice and clean.

DAN. That's fine. My lady friend, Nell Polish, usually buffs my nails for me — she's a manicurist at Kitty Litter's Coiffure Salon — but while I'm here, I'll have you do them.

HEDDA. Thanks. I'll do my best.

HANS. *(Now US of DAN.)* Now for your shave...

(He reaches into a smock pocket for his razor. It's not there. He pats his other pockets. No razor. He frowns then using his right index finger like a razor, he scrapes some lather from DAN's right jaw and wipes it off on his towel.)

PAT. *(Off SR.)* Psssst!

(His hand reaches in, hands HANS his razor, then withdraws. The razor is dull as a butter knife, for safety precautions.)

HERR KUTTER, THE BARBARIC BARBER

HANS. *(Sotto voice.)* Thanks!

(He proceeds to shave DAN, again crossing DS to block DAN from the audience as he removes the lather and wipes it on the towel.)

DAN. Herr Kutter, Miss Wood, will I see you two at the Hair Ball?

HANS. I beg your pardon?

DAN. Miss Litter is having a ball...

HEDDA. *(Cutting in.)* Everyone's entitled to a good time.

DAN. I mean a dance. I plan to escort Nell to it.

HANS. Dat's duh first I've heard of it.

DAN. I'm sure you'll receive an invitation. Nell said every barber and beautician in the city will get one.

HANS. *(Turning to the audience.)* Vhat luck! I've seen duh old dame und her lovely niece in duh society columns. Dis vill be a golden opportunity for me to meet dem und sveep duh girl off her feet! Den I plan to...

PAT. *(Off SR.) (Cutting in.)* You already told them that.

HANS. Oh, yeah. *(Turning back to face DAN and completing the shave.)* A Hair Ball, eh? Miss Vood und I vill certainly attend. Dere — all finished.

(He steps to SL of DAN. We see DAN's shaved face with half his moustache missing. HANS does a startled take.)

HEDDA. Hey! What happened to...

HANS. *(Cutting in.)* Duh time! You're right, Hedda — ve had better hurry Officer Druff along before our next customer arrives! Here, let me get duh rest of duh shave cream off your face! *(He pats his pocket, finds a pencil, and takes it out. He crosses below DAN, his back to the audience, wipes the remaining lather off DAN's face*

HERR KUTTER, THE BARBARIC BARBER

with the clean side of the towel, then quickly draws the now missing piece of DAN's moustache back on with the pencil. <Use an eyebrow pencil if needed.> HEDDA watches, amazed. HANS moves to SL of DAN, replacing the pencil in his pocket.) All done!

(He removes the cape. DAN stands. HANS lays the cape across the back of the chair then holds out his hand SL. STAGEHAND's hand comes in from off SL and hands HANS DAN's uniform coat. It is heavily sprinkled with white dots -- dandruff. HANS holds the coat for DAN who puts it on.)

DAN. How much do I owe you?
HANS. Shave and a haircut — two bits.

(DAN takes some coins from his pocket, gives one to HANS, and puts one in HEDDA's bowl.)

DAN. Thanks, Herr Kutter. There's nothing more refreshing than a good, close shave.

HEDDA. *(An aside.)* Anytime Hans comes near anyone with a razor, they're in for a close shave.

DAN. It's almost time for me to report for duty. I'll see you two at the ball. Until Saturday... *(He EXITS SL and changes into his gala outfit.)*

HANS. It von't be hard to spot him at duh ball — he alvays looks like he's valked through a room vhere a plaster ceiling vas falling down.

HEDDA. Can't cha do something to help Officer Druff with his problem? He's really flaky.

HANS. *(To the audience.)* Talk about duh pot calling duh kettle black. *(To HEDDA.)* Help him? Short of scalping him, no. But who cares about dat? Ve haf bigger fish to fly.

HERR KUTTER, THE BARBARIC BARBER

HEDDA. You mean "fry".

HANS. Don't be zuch a nit-picker! You are alvays picking nits!

HEDDA. I am not!

HANS. You are too! Before you came along, duh place vas full of nits, but not any more! You picked dem all!

HEDDA. *(Staring at him.)* I see one nit — a nitwit.

HANS. *(Sarcastically.)* Oh, ha-ha. I suppose you tink you're really comical.

HEDDA. *(An aside.)* Somebody in this play has to be.

HANS. *(Shooting her a look.)* As I vas saying, ve haf bigger fish to "fry".

HEDDA. What kind of fish are you talking about? I thought I'd ask, just for the halibut.

(She giggles giddily at her joke.)

HANS. Keep it clean! Dis iss a family show!

HEDDA. Sorry.

HANS. *(Sotto voice; no accent.)* Now you've done it — I can't remember my next line.

HEDDA. *(Sotto voice.)* Don't blame me. I've known rocks with a better memory than yours.

PAT. *(ENTERS SR carrying an open script. A piece of tape now covers the tear in his shirt sleeve.)* Uh...excuse me... I saw you through your window and wondered if you can help me find Central Park. I got this "map"...

(He shows HANS the script. HANS frantically searches for his next line.)

HANS. *(Muttering under his breath.)* "...bigger fish to fly"..."you mean fry"..."zuch a nit-picker..." *(To PAT.)* Okay, I got it. *(PAT shakes*

HERR KUTTER, THE BARBARIC BARBER

the script at him, impatient.) Oh! Central Park! It's duh green blob right dere!

PAT. Thanks. I'm leaving now. *(He EXITS SL. Off SL.)* How did I do? Do you think the audience bought it?

HANS. *(Shooting a look off SL.)* As I vas saying before dat man in duh very strange clothing came in, ve haf to make plans. Dan Druff said duh ball is Saturday; Saturday vill be here before you know it.

HEDDA. You could be right; I'm not even sure what today is. What do we have to do by Saturday?

HANS. Get me a new tuxedo *(or suit)*...maybe a facial...exercise a little to tone up... I must be in tip-top shape if I'm going to make Miss Lorrie Ell fall madly in love vid me!

HEDDA. In tip-top shape... By Saturday, huh?

HANS. Vhat's duh matter? Don't you tink I can pull it off?

HEDDA. *(An aside.)* The only thing I've seen him pull off is half of Officer Druff's moustache. *(To HANS.)* Yeah, boss...I'm sure you can do it...there's no question about it. .maybe...

HANS. Dat's settled, den. Come! Ve go shopping! *(They start off SL. They will remove their smocks and HANS will don his suit coat. The lights fade to blackout. The cape is struck from the chair and it is returned to its former position. The shaving mug is struck and the table and stool are placed SR of the SR curtain UC. Off SL in the dark:)* That wasn't my fault! *(HEDDA's real first name)* threw me!

HEDDA. *(Off SL.)* I'll throw you, all right! I'll throw you into the orchestra pit if you keep blaming me for your incompetence!

HANS. *(Off SL.)* Incompetence?!?

HEDDA. *(Off SL.)* You heard me. I hear they're going to declare a "Be Kind to Lame-Brains Week" in your honor.

HANS. *(Off SL.)* Why, you...

PAT. *(Off SL, cutting in.)* Quit bickering, you two! Just keep the

HERR KUTTER, THE BARBARIC BARBER

play going!

Scene 6
Harry's Barber Shop. Later that morning.

(The curtain opens and the lights fade up SL. HARRY sits in the chair, holding the invitation, a dreamy expression on his face. BARBARA POLE and SHU [SHUBERT] SHINER ENTER UC through the SL curtain. BARBARA, 20's, is Harry's manicurist, a good-natured girl. SHU, 20's, is his shoeshine man. He's a nice guy who likes to joke around.)

BARBARA. We're back from the suppliers.
SHU. We stocked up on shoe shine supplies for my clients...
BARBARA. And I got some new nail clippers and files for mine.
SHU. Did you have many customers while we were gone?

(HARRY continues to stare into space. BARBARA shakes his arm, bringing him back to reality.)

HARRY. Huh...what...?
BARBARA. Shu asked you if you've had many clients this morning?
HARRY. I had one...well, she wasn't really a client...
SHU. She?
BARBARA. A woman?
HARRY. A girl... A beautiful young girl...

HERR KUTTER, THE BARBARIC BARBER

HEDDA. *(Off DR.)* Talk about miscasting...
HARRY. She came in about a Hair Ball.
BARBARA. Was she choaking?
HEDDA. *(Off DR.)* I wish.
HARRY. Not that kind of hairball — this kind of Hair Ball.

(He hands them the invitation which they read.)

BARBARA. A dance! Oh, boy!
SHU. Are we invited too?
HARRY. Yes. It's for me and my employees, Barbara Pole and Shubert Shiner.
SHU. Barbara and Shu, that's us.
BARBARA. It's being hosted by Miss Kitty Litter. Wow! Are you going to invite a girl to go with you, Harry?
SHU. That would make her one Harry date.

(He guffaws at his joke.)

HARRY. A date? No. The only girl I want to be with will be there already — her niece, Miss Lorrie Ell, who brought the invitation.
BARBARA. Oh, ho... I'm beginning to get the picture... Shu, notice the faraway look in Harry's eye, the little smile on his lips, the dreamy tone of his voice... I think Harry has fallen in love.
SHU. I figured it was either that, or somebody had bounced a brick off his head. 'Fess up, pal — is it love, or have you got a concussion?
HARRY. *(A really dreamy expression.)* It's love — definately love!

(STAGEHAND rings the triangle off SL.)

HERR KUTTER, THE BARBARIC BARBER

HANS. *(Off SL.)* Who do you think you are? Tinkerbell? *(The ringing stops.)*

BARBARA. Who are you going to take to the ball, Shu?

SHU. Myself. I'm the only one I can think of to ask who'll say yes. How about you?

BARBARA. I'm not dating anyone, either. I guess I'll go alone.

SHU. I know — let's go together. While we're there, maybe you'll meet a nice, single barber, and I'll meet an available beautician or manicurist.

BARBARA. It's a deal. *(They shake hands.)*

SHU. You know, Barbara, there's just one thing I dread about falling in love.

BARBARA. What's that, Shu?

SHU. *(Looking at HARRY.)* It sure puts a goofy look on your face.

(BARBARA giggles. The lights fade out and the curtain closes.)

KITTY. *(Off DL.)* My mirror! I need my mirror!
LORRIE. *(Off DL.)* It's broken.
KITTY. *(Off DL.)* What am I supposed to do!?!
PAT. *(Off DL.)* Get ready to go on — I'll think of something!

(STAGEHAND ENTERS DL and puts the mirror frame, now without a mirror, DL. BARBARA, HARRY and SHU change into their gala outfits. Stagehands convert the main set into the ballroom: they move the screens UL and UR to in front of the barber shop and salon, hiding them; as they do this, they reverse them so that their glittery sides face out. The remove the curtains at the doorways UC, reverse them, them hang them with with the glittery sides out. They open the doors SL and SR and

HERR KUTTER, THE BARBARIC BARBER

cover the openings with two more glittery curtains.)

Scene 7
Kitty's home. That afternoon.

(The area light DL fades up in front of the main curtain. STAGEHAND freezes, giving the audience a startled look. He backs slowly backward till he's offstage. KITTY and LORRIE ENTER DL and move to where KITTY is at the mirror, LORRIE SR of her.)

KITTY. *(As they ENTER.)* It's been an exhausting day, but...

(Her voice trails off as she stops and watches, aghast, as PAT ENTERS DL PUSHING HEDDA in front of him till she is SL of the mirror frame.)

HEDDA. *(Sotto voice.)* This is ridiculous! I can't...
PAT. *(Sotto voice; nodding at the audience.)* They'll never notice. Just do it!

(He EXITS SL. HEDDA faces KITTY through the frame and matches her body position. For the rest of the scene, first HEDDA, then STAGEHAND, will pretend to be reflections. Their comic mimes should be the highlight of the scene.)

KITTY. *(Mutters under her breath.)* Why did he put that egotis-

HERR KUTTER, THE BARBARIC BARBER

tical actress there? *(Out loud.)* Uh...as I was saying, it's been an exhausting day. Will you help me with my coat, dear?
    LORRIE. Of course, Aunt Kitty.

(LORRIE helps KITTY who is facing the mirror take off the coat. HEDDA matches KITTY's movements.)

    KITTY. And my hat. *(She takes it off and hands it to LORRIE, HEDDA miming the hat.)*
    LORRIE. I love your dress.
    KITTY. Why, thank you. I love it, too. *(She paces around, checking her reflection; HEDDA matches her moves.)* I hope it doesn't look too youthful for me. *(Stares into mirror, her face inches from HEDDA's.)* I think I notice some wrinkles that I never saw before.

(HEDDA is outraged. She puts her hands to the sides of her face and pushes inward, making wrinkles on her face.)

    LORRIE. I'm sure it's just your imagination. I'll bet the next time you look in a mirror, they'll be gone.
    KITTY. No doubt you're right. It's not me that's old, it's the mirror.

(She steps SR from the mirror, just in time to avoid being kicked by HEDDA who thrusts a foot through the frame at KITTY's rear. KITTY takes her hat and coat from LORRIE.)

    LORRIE. That's what it is. *(She crosses SL past KITTY to the mirror.)* Why, it makes me look like an old hag! *(She turns and flits SR a couple of steps as HEDDA thrusts her hands through the frame toward LORRIE's throat.)*
    PAT. *(Off DL.)* Get her!

HERR KUTTER, THE BARBARIC BARBER

(STAGEHAND STUMBLES IN DL, as if pushed, and grabs HEDDA.)

HEDDA. I don't have to take this! You want a reflection in the mirror? YOU be it!

(She STORMS OFF DL.)

KITTY. I meant to tell you, I like your new dress, too, Lorrie.
LORRIE. It is nice, isn't it? *(She turns back to the mirror. She's startled to see STAGEHAND, but quickly regains her composure. STAGEHAND will desperately try to match LORRIE's moves.)* I love the way it moves. *(She holds out her skirt and twists around. STAGEHAND mimes the same.)* It makes me feel very girlish. *(She giggles, putting a hand to her mouth. Ditto STAGEHAND. Playing with her hair.)* I'm glad I wore it today. I met a very nice young man.
KITTY. Really? Who?
LORRIE. A barber to whom I delivered an invitation. Harry Noggin. He said he'll attend the ball. *(She turns back to face KITTY. STAGEHAND turns his back to the frame, but looks over his shoulder at LORRIE.)*
KITTY. Then I look forward to meeting him there.

(LORRIE will cross to KITTY. STAGEHAND will cross away from his side of the mirror. Once he's near the edge of the stage, he HURRIES OFF DL.)

LORRIE. Harry seems like a real gentleman. I hope you will like him.
KITTY. If you do, I'm sure I shall as well. I bet my little kitties have missed me. Why don't we go give them a cuddle?
LORRIE. *(With a glance back at the empty frame.)* I'd love to.

HERR KUTTER, THE BARBARIC BARBER

(They EXIT DL as the lights fade out. The mirror is struck. LORRIE and KITTY change into their ball gowns.)

HANS. *(Off DL.)* That's was the dumbest thing I've ever seen.
HEDDA. *(Off DL.)* You want to see something dumber? Go find a real mirror and look in it!

(HANS and HEDDA change into their gala outfits.)

Scene 8
Various New York locations. Saturday night.

(The following vignettes take place in front of the main curtain as the set continues to be changed behind it. The area light DR fades up. NELL ENTERS DR, dressed for the ball.)

NELL. *(To DAN, Off DR.)* Come on, Dan. We don't want to be late for the ball.
DAN. *(Off DR.)* Ah, Nell, I'll be the only man there who's dressed like this.
NELL. I don't care, it's the perfect choice for you. I think you look great in it.
DAN. *(Off DR.)* If you say so.

(He ENTERS DR, wearing a white tuxedo [or suit]. The other half of his moustache is gone as is the drawn in half.)

HERR KUTTER, THE BARBARIC BARBER

NELL. *(Adjusting his bow tie.)* Trust me, Dan — until they find a cure for dandruff, white is definately your color.

DAN. This outfit will stand out like a spotlight. At least you'll be able to find me in a crowd.

NELL. Honey, I could find you anywhere; you leave a trail of flakes like Hansel and Gretel left bread crumbs. I look down at the floor where you've been and say to myself, "Well, that's just Dan all over."

DAN. You're a great gal, Nell. Not every girl could love a guy who can shake his head and create a blizzard.

NELL. It's not that bad.

DAN. Oh, yeah?

(He shakes his head. STAGEHAND's hand comes out DR, tosses a handful of tiny white confetti into the air around DAN's head, then withdraws.)

NELL. I stand corrected. I guess I could put a fish bowl over your head and make a snow globe...but that's okay, dear — I like snow globes.

DAN. And I like you. *(He hugs her, then offers his arm.)* Shall we? *(She links her arm in his.)* There's a certain barber I hope to see at the ball. We need to have a little discussion about my moustache.

NELL. Your missing moustache.

DAN. Exactly. I'll have to be careful -- I guess my new tux [or suit] wouldn't look so hot with blood on it.

(They EXIT DR as the area light fades out. BOO and BEA ENTER DL. They are dressed in their ball gowns. The area light DL fades up.)

HERR KUTTER, THE BARBARIC BARBER

BEA. *(SL of BOO.)* I've been looking...

(Her comment trails off as she sees, in the spill from her area light, STAGEHAND's arms appear from behind the proscenium DR. He is holding a broom. BOO turns and watches also as STAGEHAND begins to sweep the tiny confetti from the previous vignette to off DR.)

BOO. *(Mutters to herself.)* I don't believe this...
PAT. *(Off DL.)* Leave it!

(STAGEHAND's arms freeze a beat, then he gives the broom a few more frantic sweeps before he whisks the broom out of sight.)

BOO. You were saying, Bea...?
BEA. I've been looking forward to tonight's ball all week.
BOO. Me, too — and what a hectic week it was! I've never trimmed as many heads as I did the last five days. I inhaled so much hair I could spit curls!
BEA. I know what you mean. By the end of each day we were both covered with so much of it we looked like the Abomninable Snow-women! But tonight! — tonight we look glamorous!
BOO. Do you really think so?
BEA. I know so.
BOO. Oh, good. I would have been happy with "nice"...or even "clean".
BEA. I think it was a good idea for us to pool our week's tips so we could hire a horse-drawn hansom cab to take us to the ball, rather than ride on the trolley car.
BOO. Oh, so do I. Can you imagine the stares we'd get on the trolley, dressed in these gowns?
BEA. The same kind of looks Cinderella would have got if she

HERR KUTTER, THE BARBARIC BARBER

had hiked up her skirts and walked to her ball, probably.

BOO. I love that fairy tale. If only I could meet my Prince Charming at Miss Kitty's gala.

BEA. You never know, Boo — it could happen. *(Off DL PAT makes a weak neighing sound.)* I think our cab has arrived. Shall we?

BOO. Lead the way, Bea.

(They EXIT DL as the area light fades out.)

BEA. *(Off DL.)* What the heck was that supposed to be?

PAT. *(Off DL.)* A horse. I couldn't get the sound effect tape of a horse whinnying to work, so I improvised.

BOO. *(Off DL.)* Some improvisation — it sounded like your horse was about to fall over dead.

PAT. *(Off DL.)* Just take your places for your next scene!

BEA. *(Off DL.)* Okay...okay...

BOO. *(Off DL.)* What a grouch...

(MINNIE and LOTTA ENTER DR in their ball gowns. They have purses. MINNIE'S purse is on a small chain; she will keep it on her left wrist in this and the ballroom scenes. The area light DR fades up.)

LOTTA. I appreciate your asking me to come over and ride to the ball with you and Holder, Minnie.

MINNIE. You're welcome, Lotta. He should be down shortly. And they say that women are slow getting dressed. Honestly!

LOTTA. I can't wait to see what all of the women are wearing tonight. I've got a pad and pencil in here. *(Indicates her purse.)* I plan to take lots of notes so I can describe everyone's gowns in my column... including yours, of course. It's lovely.

HERR KUTTER, THE BARBARIC BARBER

MINNIE. Thank you — so is yours. I have something in my purse, too. I'll let you in on a little secret if you promise not to tell Kitty beforehand. I want to surprise her when she announces her new charity at the ball.

LOTTA. I swear I'll not breathe a word! What is it?

MINNIE. *(Opens her purse and pulls an envelope halfway out.)* I'm going to give her this. Inside the envelope are ten one hundred dollar bills.

LOTTA. Oh, my goodness!

MINNIE. Occasionally, Holder's bank donates money to good causes. When I told him about the shelter for homeless cats Kitty proposes to build, he said we can do our part by giving her this to get her project started.

LOTTA. How generous!

MINNIE. Kitty has accounts for all of her salons at Holder's bank. I guess he wants to show a good customer his appreciation.

LOTTA. A thousand dollars! That's a lot of appreciation! Kitty will be thrilled.

MINNIE. Remember — mum's the word.

LOTTA. Don't worry — I won't let the cat out of the bag. Now I can't wait to get to the ball.

MINNIE. Me, neither. Let's get our coats. We're leaving, even if I have to drag Holder along in his longjohns!

(LOTTA giggles as they EXIT DR and the area light fades out as the area light DL fades up. HANS ENTERS DL, now dressed for the ball.)

HANS. I'll need you to... *(He stops, then turns back SL. A harsh whisper: The real first name of the actress playing HEDDA.)*! Where are you!?!

HEDDA. *(Off DL.)* I'm here offstage where you should be. We

HERR KUTTER, THE BARBARIC BARBER

don't come on until the scene after next.
   HANS. Oh.

(He EXITS DL. The light fades out, then fades back up. HARRY ENTERS DL, FOLLOWED BY BARBARA and SHU. All are dressed in their gala outfits.)

HARRY. I've counted the moments until tonight...
   SHU. *(Joking.)* All week? I bet it comes to a really big number!
   BARBARA. *(Good-naturedly.)* Don't be a wise guy. Go on, Harry.
   HARRY. I can't believe it's finally here — the night I get to see Lorrie again.
   BARBARA. I'm anxious to meet her.
   SHU. So am I. It's obvious this Lorrie Ell holds Harry's heart in her hands.
   HEDDA. *(Off DL.)* Yuck! That sounds gross!
   PAT. *(Off DL.)* Shuuu!
   HARRY. I cannot deny that I have fallen under her spell. She is the loveliest mortal I have ever seen.
   HEDDA. *(STEPPING IN DL; to the audience.)* Is there an optomitrist in the house?

(PAT reaches from offstage and PULLS HER OFF.)

   SHU. Why don't we go into the building and find the ballroom?
   BARBARA. *(Looking off DL.)* Yeah — there are some really strange people out here on the street. *(They start walking to DR. The other lights on the forestage fade up.)* Harry, are you sure Miss Ell doesn't already have a suitor?
   SHU. Good question. She's the niece of a very wealthy woman. A lot of men would court her for that reason alone.

HERR KUTTER, THE BARBARIC BARBER

HARRY. *(Frowns.)* I hadn't thought of that... She seemed to like me, and she said she looked forward to seeing me at the ball.

SHU. Are you sure she didn't say she looked forward to seeing you bald?

BARBARA. *(Elbowing him in the ribs.)* You're awful! He's just teasing you, Harry, because he's jealous; Shu wishes he could meet a girl to fall for as hard as you've fallen for Lorrie Ell.

SHU. Guilty. Who knows? Tonight might be the night. Let's go find out.

(They EXIT DR. The lights fade out, then the area light DL fades back up.)

HANS. *(Off DL.)* Now?
HEDDA. *(Off DL.)* Now.

(They ENTER DL, dressed for the ball.)

HANS. I'll need you to keep your eyes und ears open at the ball tonight.

HEDDA. You mean like this?

(She opens her eyes wide and leans left, then right, as if listening to something.)

HANS. I vas speaking metaphorically, Hedda.
HEDDA. Really? I didn't know you knew a foreign language.
HANS. Vhat I meant vas, pay attention to duh udder people dere. You saw how attractive Lorrie Ell is when she brought our invitation. *(HEDDA gives a sour look.)* Help me find out if I haf any competition for her affections. If dere are any udder men who attempt to court her, I'll haf to crush dem underfoot.

HERR KUTTER, THE BARBARIC BARBER

HEDDA. You are so...barbaric.

HANS. I tink ve've already established dat.

HEDDA. Oh, yeah. If Miss Ell does have other suitors, how do you plan to...what you just said?

HANS. Dat's vhere you come in. It's your job to distract dem vhile I make my play for duh young heiress.

HEDDA. Distract them? How?

HANS. By using your vomanly charms. You haf "vamp" listed on your resume — so beguile dem...entice dem... You can do dat, can't you?

HEDDA. Oh, that's no problem. Vamping is my specialty. I do my vamping exercises every day, just to keep in shape. I'll show you.

[AUDIENCE PARTICIPATION SECTION — Optional]

HEDDA. *(Continued.)* It'll be easier if I have someone to practice my feminine wiles on. Can we have the house lights up? *(The house lights come up, as well as the rest of the lights on the forestage. To a man in the audience.)* You — sir? Will you come up and help me, please?

HANS. You might as vell do vhat she asks. Hedda von't quit till she gets her vay.

(HEDDA will get the man — or another, if the first one refuses — to come onto the stage. She and HANS should be prepared to improvise in character during this section. Once a man is onstage, HEDDA will ask him his name, then say:)

HEDDA. Could I have a little music to set the mood here? *(A vampy instrumental number begins. It can be modern. HEDDA does a comic mime/dance, slinking around the man, striking alluring poses and making come-hither expressions. She strikes her final pose as the music ends. To HANS.)* What do you think?

HERR KUTTER, THE BARBARIC BARBER

HANS. Dat vas okay.

HEDDA. "Okay"!?! Just "okay"!?! There's not a woman here who can vamp better than I can! I'll prove it! *(She points to three women in the audience, one at a time, and says "You! Miss? Can you come up here? How about you?" and such until she has the trio join her onstage. She asks them their names.)* You saw what I was doing when the music was playing? I want you to do the same kind of thing when I tell you to, but see if you can do it better. Let's start with you. *(She picks one woman. The music starts again. After the first woman vamps a while, HEDDA will replace her with the second woman, then replace her with the third. Near the end of the number, she'll say:)* All together now!

(HEDDA and the other two women join the one who's vamping and all four vamp the man till the number ends.)

HANS. *(To the audience.)* Okay, folks, ve need your help here. Tell us vid your applause vich woman up here is duh best vamp. Vas it vamp number von?... *(He touches the first woman's shoulder.)*... vamp number two?... *(Same business.)* ... vamp number tree... *(Same business.)* ... or our own Hedda Vood? *(Same business.)* Duh vinner iss *(Gives name.)* Tank you for your help in selecting her. Ve haf some prizes for duh contestants. *(STAGEHAND's hands come out from the edge of the proscenium DL, holding prizes. HANS and HEDDA give them to the women.)* Und a gift for duh gentleman as vell. *(The man is given a gift.)* You may go back to your seats now. *(The audience members return to their seats.)* You can take down duh extra lights. *(The house lights and all but the DL area light fade out.)*

HEDDA. *(If she wins the contest, she says)* See? I told you I'm the best! *(If she doesn't win, she says:)* That really wasn't fair! I think that woman is a professional!

HERR KUTTER, THE BARBARIC BARBER

[END OF AUDIENCE PARTICIPATION SECTION]

HANS. *(If the audience participation section is omitted, HEDDA strikes some vamp poses before HANS says)* You've made your point, Hedda. If ve don't hurry up, duh ball vill be over before ve get dere.

HEDDA. *(Linking her arm through his.)* I'm ready when you are, Hans.

(They EXIT DL as the light fades out.)

HANS. *(Off DL.)* Come on, *(Says Hedda's real first name)*, we've to to get to our next entrance. *(Beat.)* What are you waiting for?

PAT. *(Off DL.)* Let go of my hand.

HANS. *(Off DL.)* Sorry. It's really dark back here.

Scene 9
The Hair Ball. Shortly after.

(The curtain opens and the lights fade up on the ball. Onstage are BEA, BOO, NELL and DAN SR; KITTY and LORRIE CS; MINNIE and LOTTA SL. EXTRAS, if used, mill around US. You might consider dressing female extras as men to be dance partners. All ad-lib quietly. The women are dressed in gowns. Ideally, the men will wear tuxedos, but dark suits will do, if necessary. Make sure the men's clothes are consistant — all tuxes or all suits. The exception is DAN whose outfit is white, as we've

HERR KUTTER, THE BARBARIC BARBER

already seen.)

BEA. You look very dapper tonight, Dan.

DAN. I appreciate that. I think I look like a skinny snowman.

BOO. I think your tuxedo *(or suit)* is very chic. I'm glad you were able to get off duty so you could escort Nell to the gala.

DAN. My chief is a pretty understanding fella, plus he thought it would be a good idea to have a policeman on the premises since all the women here will be wearing their finest jewelry.

BOO. My goodness! Does he think someone might attempt to rob us!?!

DAN. There's probably little danger of that, but it never hurts to be cautious.

NELL. Well, you can keep one eye out for wrongdoers, but the other eye had better be on me!

DAN. Yes, dear. Don't worry — you'll get my almost completely undivided attention.

LOTTA. Where did Holder disappear to, Minnie?

MINNIE. Who knows? He had just better return in time for the dancing. I feel like sweeping around the ballroom floor tonight.

(STAGEHAND's arms thrust through the curtained doorway SL. He is holding a broom. LOTTA and MINNIE react, surprised.)

PAT *(Offstage, behind the SL doorway.)* That's not what she meant, dummy! *(STAGEHAND pulls the broom offstage.)* Where's the actor who plays Holder? Help me find him!

LOTTA. I wouldn't mind a dance later, myself.

MINNIE. I don't doubt there will be any number of eligible bachelors here who would be happy to be your partner, Lotta.

LOTTA. That would be nice...as long as no one attempts to sweep me off my feet. *(She shoots a look at the DL doorway.)* In the mean-

HERR KUTTER, THE BARBARIC BARBER

time, I'll take some notes for my column.

(She takes a pad and pencil from her purse and mimes conferring with MINNIE as she takes notes. HANS and HEDDA ENTER through the curtained doorway SL.)

HEDDA. Wow! What a swanky place! That Miss Litter must really be loaded!
HANS. Vhat did you expect, a couple of streamers und some vilted carnations? I told you she's rich. Dere she iss over dere, vid my future bride, Miss Lorrie Ell.
HEDDA. *(Sourly.)* So I see.

(HARRY, BARBARA and SHU ENTER through the curtained doorway SR.)

HARRY. Here we are...
BARBARA. Gee, what an elegant ballroom!
SHU. The people don't look too shabby, either.
HARRY. There's our hostess, Miss Kitty Litter, in the *(color)* dress, and with her is the love of my life, Lorrie Ell!
LORRIE. *(Spotting HARRY.)* Aunt Kitty, he's here — Harry Noggin, the man of my dreams!

(STAGEHAND's hands thrust in DL, holding the triangle. He tinkles it.)

HANS. *(Shooting STAGEHAND a look, sarcastically, no accent.)* I hate to tell you, but the parade turned left at the last corner. *(STAGEHAND quickly pulls the triangle off. To HEDDA, back in character.)* Come on. *(He leads her to KITTY and LORRIE, CS.)* Ah, Miss Ell. May I say how lovely you look tonight?...*(He kisses*

HERR KUTTER, THE BARBARIC BARBER

her hand.)...even lovelier dan vhen you delivered our invitation last Monday, if dat's possible.

LORRIE. *(Sotto voice, to KITTY.)* Now I'll have to wash my hand with disinfectant. *(Though trying to appear pleasant, the actors' underlying hostility toward one another shows through.)* Thank you, Herr Kutter. Aunt Kitty, may I introduce Herr Hans Kutter, and his manicurist, Hedda...cabbage?

HEDDA. Wood! My name is Hedda Wood!

LORRIE. My mistake. I knew it was something you might find in a compost heap.

KITTY. Charmed to meet you, Herr Kutter...Miss Compost — I mean, Wood.

HANS. It iss our pleasure, Miss Litter.

(He kisses her hand.)

KITTY. *(Sotto voice, to LORRIE.)* Save some Lysol for me.

HANS. *(Under his breath to HEDDA.)* Remind me to gargle later.

HEDDA. *(Under her breath.)* Remind me to strangle both of them later.

PAT. *(Off SL; a harsh whisper.)* Ladies — shake hands!

(HEDDA shakes hands with KITTY and LORRIE. All look as if they're handling snakes.)

SHU. Hey, Harry, who's that man who was slobbering over your ladylove's hand?

HARRY. His name is Hans Kutter. I don't care for him. I met him at a barbers' convention once. He's from Germany.

SHU. That explains the hand kissing stuff. European men do that a lot. I think it's silly.

HERR KUTTER, THE BARBARIC BARBER

BARBARA. I think it's romantic.
SHU. Yeah? Hear that, Harry? Barbara thinks it's romantic to have some guy drool spit on a gal's knuckles. *(She nudges him.)* Ouch!
BARBARA. It wouldn't hurt you to learn some manners if you want to impress some young lady tonight.
SHU. I've got good manners... I just can't remember where I left 'em.
LORRIE. If you'll excuse me, I see someone I must speak to.

(She crosses to HARRY.)

HANS. But...
KITTY. I, too, need to confer with a guest. Do enjoy yourselves.

(She crosses to MINNIE and LOTTA.)

HANS. Vhat's der problem? I took a bath.
HEDDA. The next time you might consider using soap.
LORRIE. Good evening, Harry.
HARRY. Good evening, Lorrie.

(The shake hands. STAGEHAND thrusts out the triangle again and plays it.)

HANS. *(To STAGEHAND; No accent.)* That's it! No more tinkling! If you do that one more time, I'll come off there and break your tinkler!

(STAGEHAND quickly withdraws the triangle.)

HARRY. Lorrie Ell, these are my employees, Barbara Pole and

HERR KUTTER, THE BARBARIC BARBER

Shubert Shiner.
    LORRIE. It's a pleasure to meet you.

(They shake hands and ad-lib greetings.)

    SHU. Call me Shu, Miss Ell. Everyone does.
    LORRIE. And I'm Lorrie.
    BARBARA. If you'll excuse us, Lorrie, we'll leave you two alone while we mingle.
    SHU. We will?
    BARBARA. We will.

(She pulls SHU to SR where they join BEA, BOO, NELL and DAN; all mime introducing themselves.)

    HANS. Drat! Miss Ell is talking to duh Noggin boy. I need to hear vhat de're saying.
    HEDDA. If you had washed your ears while you were taking that bath...
    HANS. Oh, shut up. Stroll vid me dat vay. Act casual.

(She links her arm in his. They stroll to near HARRY and LORRIE with exaggerated nonchalance.)

    HARRY. I saw you talking with Herr Kutter. Are you...um...close friends?
    LORRIE. Heavens, no. I met him only last Monday when I delivered his invitation to the ball...the same day I met you.
    HARRY. I suppose it's impossible to feel close to someone after just one meeting, isn't it? Or do you think it is?
    LORRIE. Oh, I don't know... If two people...a boy and a girl... were really meant for each other, who's to say they couldn't realize

HERR KUTTER, THE BARBARIC BARBER

it instantly?

HARRY. I believe they could. I think that's what the romantics call "love at first sight".

LORRIE. That's what they call it, all right.

HARRY. I'd like to discuss that phenomenon with you further. If only there was some quiet little corner where we could be alone...

LORRIE. Perhaps the veranda off the ballroom? There's a bench there and a gentle breeze and moonlight...

HARRY. It sounds perfect. Where...?

LORRIE. Come, I'll show you.

(She takes his hand and leads him to UC where they EXIT through one of the doorways. As this happens:)

HEDDA. They're holding hands!

HANS. I know! I saw!...und all that blather about "love at first sight"... She seems smitten vid duh lad!

HEDDA. So what are you going to do?

HANS. I must eavesdrop further on dere conversation. Den I'll decide. I'll go around duh side to duh veranda. You stay here und circulate.

HEDDA. I can do that.

(She moves to the group SR and mimes talking with them.)

HANS. *(To the audience.)* I haven't forgot about you, but I've got my hands full at duh moment. I'll talk to you later!

(He EXITS QUICKLY through the doorway SR.)

KITTY. I believe I'll have the musicians play a few selections; some of the guests might like to dance.

HERR KUTTER, THE BARBARIC BARBER

LOTTA. Musicians? I don't see any musicians.
KITTY. They're up there, in the musicians' gallery above the ballroom. See?

(She points upward.)

LOTTA. Oh... How quaint.
KITTY. Excuse me.

(She EXITS throught the doorway SL.)

MINNIE. If there's going to be dancing, Holder had better get here soon...*(Shooting a look at the SL doorway.)*... if he knows what's good for him!
KITTY. *(Off SL.)* You heard her! Where's the actor playing Holder!?!
PAT. *(Off SL.)* I can't find him! He didn't show up!
KITTY. *(Off SL.)* Well, somebody had better get out there! And Lotta needs a partner, too!
PAT. *(Off SL.)* Okay...uh...you!...here!...put this on!
STAGEHAND. *(Off SL.)* Huh?

(Unnoticed by MINNIE and LOTTA, HEDDA has drifted to SR of them and will overhear their conversation.)

MINNIE. After the musical portion of the evening is over, I hope Kitty makes the announcement about her charity. I can't wait to give her this thousand dollars I've got for her.

(She pulls the envelope partly was out of her purse, then puts it back. HEDDA is surprised, naturally.)

HERR KUTTER, THE BARBARIC BARBER

LOTTA. She'll be astonished. Make sure you don't let your purse out of your sight.
MINNIE. I won't, even though I can't believe there would be any thieves at a society function such as this.
LOTTA. You never know.

(If LOTTA is included in the dance, she puts her pad and pencil in her purse at this point.)

HEDDA. *(Softly, to herself.)* A thousand dollars! Wait till I tell Hans! We're rubbing elbows with high society tonight!

(She crosses US and EXITS through the UL doorway. An instrumental number starts to play, a piano or combo. It's a number suitable for the era such as "Bicycle Built for Two" or "Bird in a Guilded Cage"; the actors can waltz to either.)

BOO. Music! I love to dance! I wish I had a partner.
SHU. *(Bowing.)* May I offer my services, Boo?
BOO. I'd be delighted, Shu.

(They begin to dance, as do DAN and NELL. If EXTRAS are used, they will also dance. EXTRA MEN or EXTRA WOMEN dressed as men can partner BEA and BARBARA; if not, they can hold their skirts and sway.)

LOTTA. I don't think Holder is...

(PAT BURSTS THOROUGH the doorway SL, PULLING STAGEHAND with him. Both have added tux or suit coats to their modern clothes.)

HERR KUTTER, THE BARBARIC BARBER

PAT. I'm here! *(LOTTA and MINNIE are startled.)* I brought...uh...a friend to dance with Miss Scribbles.

(He grabs MINNIE and begins to dance her around awkwardly. STAGEHAND, terrified to be onstage, starts to exit SL, but KITTY ENTERS there, blocking his way.)

KITTY. *(Through clenched teeth.)* Dance with her!

(LOTTA grabs STAGEHAND and they start to dance. He tries comically to keep his face hidden from the audience. Unless an EXTRA asks KITTY to dance, she will watch the others from SL. The curtains close in a couple of feet on each side as the the music fades to low, the lights in the ballroom fade to dim, and blue moonlight fades up on the forestage. During the next scene on the veranda, we'll continue to see the dancers through the opening in the curtain, dimly.)

Scene 10
The veranda. Immediately following.

(HANS ENTERS DL and leans against the proscenium, catching his breath.)

HANS. *(To the audience.)* If I knew I could run dat fast, I vould have entered duh Olympics! I vill hide behind dat potted plant next to duh bench, und... *(He notices there is no plant or bench. Paniced — no accent.)* The plant! The bench!

HERR KUTTER, THE BARBARIC BARBER

(PAT is dancing MINNIE near the curtain opening DC.)

PAT. *(To HANS, a harsh whisper.)* You'll have to get them — I'm dancing!
MINNIE. *(Under her breath.)* That's debatable.
HANS. *(Whispering back.)* Where's the stagehand!?! *(PAT and MINNIE dance away as STAGEHAND and LOTTA immediately dance to the opening. STAGEHAND shrugs at HANS.)* Oh.
LORRIE. *(Off DR.)* The veranda is right around this corner.
HANS. Oh!

(He RUSHES OFF DL.)

HARRY. *(Off DR.)* I hear music.
LORRIE. *(Off DR.)* Yes. We can watch the dancers through the window.
HARRY. *(Off DR.)* I had much rather look at you.

(HANS RE-ENTERS carrying a potted plant which he sets DL.)

HANS. The bench! I didn't see the bench!

(LORRIE and HARRY ENTER DR, holding hands and gazing into each other's eyes. They will stroll to DL.)

HARRY. You look lovely in the moonlight, Lorrie.
LORRIE. Thank you, Harry.

(Desperate, HANS drops to his hands and knees SR of the plant, head DS, and becomes the bench. He will mutter his comments under his breath in this scene.)

HERR KUTTER, THE BARBARIC BARBER

HARRY. I'm surprised you don't have a beau, Lorrie. I mean, there must be a hundred men who would love to be your fella.

HANS. Make dat a hundred und von.

LORRIE. How sweet of you to say that, Harry. Quite a few men have attempted to court me, but I wanted to wait until I met someone special.

HARRY. Someone special?

LORRIE. Yes. And I met him last Monday It's...

HANS. Say it's me! Say it's me!

LORRIE. It's you, Harry.

HANS. Vell, crud!

HARRY. *(They stop walking.)* You...you mean you feel the same way about me as I feel about you?

LORRIE. How do you feel?

HARRY. Like I'll die if I don't do this.

(He kisses her gently.)

HANS. Dose should be my lips doing dat kissing! She's smooching duh wrong lips!

LORRIE. Golly! I was hoping you'd do that.

HANS. I vas hoping you'd drop dead!

HARRY. I've been wanting to kiss you ever since I first saw you. I've fallen in love with you, Lorrie.

LORRIE. And I, you.

HANS. Curses!

LORRIE. Goodness, I feel a little light headed.

HARRY. Why don't you sit a moment over there on that... *(For the first time, he notices HANS; surprised.)* ...bench.

(They start toward HANS.)

HERR KUTTER, THE BARBARIC BARBER

LORRIE. Yes, I believe I should sit on the... *(She notices HANS; surprised.)* ...bench.

HARRY. Rest yourself, Lorrie, dearest.

(LORRIE sits on HANS' back. He groans which does not please LORRIE. HARRY stands SR of them.)

HARRY. I feel honor bound to tell you that I am not a wealthy man — you saw my modest barber shop — but I work hard and make an honest living.

HANS. Oh, please! If I vanted corn, I'd go to Iowa!

HARRY. If I could, I would lay a fortune at your feet, but...

LORRIE. Say no more.

HANS. My sentiments exactly.

LORRIE. I, too, come from humble beginnings.

HANS. You've managed to eat well.

(He will sink VERY SLOOOOWLY down until he ends up lying flat on the floor. LORRIE will sink with him, of course, until she's sitting on his back with both her legs stretched out in front of her.)

LORRIE. I was brought up in a small New England town where my parents still live. When I finished school, Aunt Kitty invited me to come live with her in New York and work as her social secretary. It's been wonderful, staying in her lovely home and wearing the beautiful clothes she's bought me and eating fancy food...

HANS. Too much fancy food!

LORRIE. ...but I could be just as happy living a simple life with a loving husband at my side...

HANS. My side is killing me...to say nothing of my back!

HERR KUTTER, THE BARBARIC BARBER

LORRIE. ...a man I could look up to...*(She realizes she's getting lower.)*.. WAY up to...

(HANS finally flattens out with an "Oof!".)

HARRY. There seems to be a problem with this bench.
LORRIE. Indeed, there is. The rickety old thing has fallen apart.
HANS. You'd fall apart, too, if an elephant sat on you.
HARRY. Allow me. *(He takes her hands and helps her up.)* Shall we return to the party?
LORRIE. Let's do. You still have to meet Aunt Kitty.

(They start toward DR, holding hands.)

HARRY. Do you think she'll like me?
LORRIE. She'll love you. *(Sotto voice.)* What happened to the bench?
HARRY. *(Sotto voice.)* I don't know. I thought Hans would be behind the potted plant. I suppose *(the first name of the actor playing HANS.)* messed up again. *(They EXIT DR.)*
HANS. *(To the audience.)* That was not my fault! It was the dumb stage manager's fault! You saw what happened!
HEDDA. *(ENTERS DL.)* Hans, did you...? *(She is surprised to see him lying on the floor.)* What are you doing on the floor?
HANS. *(Sarcastic.)* I've invented a new exercise. Udder men do push-ups —I do push-downs. Dat crazy girl sat on me! You vould tink dey vould haf changed duh blocking.
HEDDA. I don't understand.
HANS. Vhy does dat not surprise me?
HEDDA. Is there anything I can do?
HANS. Yeah. Get a sponge und sop me up.
HEDDA. Huh?

HERR KUTTER, THE BARBARIC BARBER

HANS. Help me up! Help me up!

(HEDDA helps him to his feet.)

HEDDA. Did you eavesdrop on Miss Giddy Britches and the boy?

HANS. Yes. I vas in a position to hear every vord. *(He holds his back and gives the audience a pained look.)* Duh young fools tink dey're in love vid each other. I don't tink, at dis point, dat you could lure him avay from her.

HEDDA. Uh-oh. Not good for us, huh?

HANS. Your brain vorks like lightning, Hedda — here von second und gone duh next. Of course it's not good for us! It's a disaster!

HEDDA. What should we do? Have you got any ideas?

HANS. Not at duh moment, but vhen I get some, I'll lend you a couple. Help me back inside!

HEDDA. *(Taking his arm.)* There are some real fancy people in there, Hans. You won't believe what one lady — Minnie Bucks — has in her purse!

HANS. Tell me anyvay. *(They start DL.)* I forgot to get you a corsage. Here.

(He thrusts the potted plant at her. She drags it off as they EXIT DL. The moonlight fades out as the curtain opens and the stage lights and music fade back up.)

HERR KUTTER, THE BARBARIC BARBER

Scene 11
The Hair Ball. Immediately following.

(The music fades back up. After a few bars, it ends or fades out. Everyone applauds. PAT and STAGEHAND EXIT quickly through the SL doorway.)

LOTTA. Wonder where Holder and his friend are off to now?

MINNIE. *(Mutters under her breath.)* If I'm lucky, another continent. *(Out loud.)* I have no idea. If they play another number, I think I'll sit it out.

LOTTA. I know I will... *(To herself, under her breath.)* ...if I have to sit on barbed wire.

(They drift to DL. BEA, BARBARA, DAN and NELL are SR. SHU and BOO are UC.)

BEA. *(To BARBARA.)* It looks as if Boo and Mr. Shiner have found something to talk about. He's not your...?

BARBARA. Beau? No. We're friendly co-workers, but that's all. Shu was hoping to meet a nice, available young lady tonight.

NELL. And Boo was hoping to meet a nice young man. I have a feeling both of them got their wish.

(HARRY and LORRIE ENTER through a doorway UC.)

LORRIE. Now, where's Aunt Kitty...? There she is. Come on, Harry.

(They cross to KITTY CS and mime introductions. HANS and HEDDA ENTER through the SL doorway.)

HERR KUTTER, THE BARBARIC BARBER

HEDDA. This is a pretty good party. Oh, look — there's Officer Druff. Let's say hello.

HANS. *(Grabbing her arm.)* Are you crazy? He's duh last person I vant to see right now.

HEDDA. Oh, yeah — he might not be too happy about your cutting his moustache in half. At least it wasn't his ear. Remember the time you...

HANS. *(Cutting in.)* I remember! *(An aside.)* You don't need to hear about dat.

HEDDA. That poor guy couldn't hear anything after...

HANS. *(Cutting in.)* Just drop it, already! Now, vhich old dame is carrying around a thousand dollars in her handbag?

HEDDA. Mrs. Bucks? That's her over there in the *(color)* dress.

HANS. Dat's "she".

HEDDA. If you knew who it was, why did you ask me?

HANS. Dat's "she", not "her".

HEDDA. Not who?

HANS. Oh, never mind. *(An aside.)* Duh only grammar Hedda knows iss her mudder's mudder. *(To HEDDA.)* Ve haf to find a vay to slip dat money out of Mrs. Bucks' purse.

HEDDA. You're gonna steal her money?

HANS. Yes und no.

HEDDA. It that a trick answer?

HANS. I plan to take duh dough und den slip it into duh Noggin boy's coat pocket.

HEDDA. Why are you giving him the money? I thought you didn't like him.

HANS. I don't. Vhen Mrs. Bucks discovers duh thousand dollars is gone, I'll suggest Officer Druff search everyvon here. Vhen dey find duh stolen cash on duh boy, he'll be arrested und put in duh hoosegow.

HEDDA. Oh, I see! Then he'll be out of the way so you can

HERR KUTTER, THE BARBARIC BARBER

romance Miss Ell!

HANS. *(An aside.)* Dere's hope for her yet. *(To HEDDA.)* Precisely. Here's vhat ve'll do... *(They huddle and mime making plans.)*

KITTY. Are you enjoying yourself, Mr. Noggin?

HARRY. I'm having a wonderful time, Miss Litter.

KITTY. I have a feeling we'll be seeing a lot of each other in the future. Why don't you call me Kitty.

HARRY. I will if you'll call me Harry.

KITTY. Agreed. Everyone's here, so I suppose I can make my announcement.

HANS. *(Hearing this, he and HEDDA rush to KITTY.)* Excuse me, Miss Litter. I couldn't help overhear your comment. Before you proceed, I should tell you dat just now I happened to hear Mrs. Bucks comment to her friend dat she vished duh orchestra vould play another number so dat she could haf von more dance. She said her husband iss not a very good dancer...

PAT. *(Off SL.)* That's gratitude for you!

HANS. ...but she hoped a nice fellow like Mr. Noggin, here, vould ask her.

HARRY. Me? I've never even met Mrs. Bucks.

HANS. I'm only telling you vhat I heard.

HEDDA. It's true. Those very words came right out of her mouth.

KITTY. Minnie is a friend... If you wouldn't mind, Harry...

LORRIE. Do dance with her.

HARRY. I'll be happy to. Who is she?

KITTY. *(Pointing.)* Right over there.

HARRY. Excuse me. *(He crosses to MINNIE and LOTTA. KITTY signals the orchestra. Music starts. DAN and NELL, BOO and SHU, HANS and HEDDA start to dance. EXTRAS, if used, ask the other principals to dance; the rest dance among themselves. Those without partners watch the dancers.)* Pardon me? Mrs. Bucks? I'm Harry Noggin, Lorrie Ell's friend. I...uh...heard you like to dance, and

HERR KUTTER, THE BARBARIC BARBER

I...uh...thought you might consent to be my partner for this number.
  MINNIE. You seem like a nice young man. I shall be delighted, Mr. Noggin.

(They begin to dance. LOTTA takes notes if she doesn't have a partner. At some point, HARRY and MINNIE, HANS and HEDDA are dancing in place DC.)

  HANS. *(Sotto voice.)* I can almost reach her purse. Turn a little more.

(They maneuver until HANS can let go of HEDDA's right hand and reach over to MINNIE's left arm which is across HARRY's right shoulder, the purse hanging from her wrist. HANS opens her purse, slips out the envelope, then closes the purse. He slips the envelope into HARRY's coat pocket. The audience should see the exchange.)

  HANS. I did it. Move thataway. We don't vant to be near dem vhen duh theft iss discovered.

(They dance away from HARRY and MINNIE. BOO and SHU dance to DC.)

  SHU. Let's see, so far we've made dates for the next ten weeks.
  BOO. Do you want to plan the eleventh?

(They dance away. DAN and NELL dance to DC.)

  DAN. *(Spotting HANS.)* Hey! There he is!
  NELL. Who?
  DAN. That moustache wacker! Go that way! *(They dance to-*

HERR KUTTER, THE BARBARIC BARBER

ward HANS and HEDDA. HANS sees him and dances away. What follows is a comic chase as HANS and HEDDA flee from DAN and NELL, both couples dancing at top speed. DAN grabs HANS' shoulder DC as the number comes to an end.) Hold it, Herr Kutter!

(As the following takes place, KITTY will mime saying something to LORRIE who will EXIT UC.)

HANS. Officer Druff... I hadn't noticed you vere here.
DAN. Yeah, well, you probably didn't recognize me without my moustache.
HANS. Yes, dat's vhat it iss! You look so much younger vidout it! Doesn't he look younger, Hedda?
HEDDA. Huh? Sure... You look like a really tall ten year old.
HANS. *(Sotto voice, to HEDDA.)* Don't overdo it!
HEDDA. *(Sotto voice.)* The only thing overdone around here is your acting.
HANS. *(Sotto voice; no accent.)* If I had wanted a critic, I would have called the New York Times. *(If your local paper has a resident theatre critic, you can substitute his or her name for "the New York Times".)*

(LORRIE will RE-ENTER UC carrying a donation box which she'll give to KITTY. The box is a shoe box covered in decorative paper. It has a slit in the lid.)

DAN. I loved my moustache!
NELL. So did I. *(Giggles.)* It tickled when he kissed me.
DAN. *(Taking HANS' arm.)* Let's go outside where we can discuss this further in private.
KITTY. *(Crossing to CS as she claps her hands.)* Attention, everyone! I have an announcement!

HERR KUTTER, THE BARBARIC BARBER

DAN. You're not off the hook yet. *(He releases HANS.)*

HANS. *(Mutters as he rubs his arm.)* First that stage manager, then you.

(Everyone makes a semi-circle around KITTY.)

KITTY. As some of you already know, I've invited you here tonight for a purpose. It's no secret that I have a special place in my heart for cats.

HEDDA. *(Under her breath.)* It takes one to know one.

KITTY. It is my intention to establish a Kitty Litter shelter for homeless felines. I hope you will assist me. I'm going to ask each of you to place a donation box like this one in your hair salons and barber shops, and that you'll invite your customers to contribute to this worthwhile cause. *(Everyone applauds.)*

HARRY. We'll be happy to, Miss Kitty. *(The others ad-lib agreement.)*

KITTY. Thank you so much, everyone. You'll find a stack of boxes like this one at the exit, so be sure to take a Kitty Litter box with you when you leave.

MINNIE. *(Crossing to KITTY.)* If you will allow me, Kitty, Holder and I would like to contribute the first donation.

PAT. *(Off SL.)* Should I go on?

MINNIE. Since Holder has stepped out... *(Cuts her eyes to the SL doorway.)*... I'll make the donation for both of us.

KITTY. How lovely, Minnie. Everyone, this is my dear friend, Minnie Bucks.

MINNIE. On behalf of Holder's bank...*(Opens her purse.)*... please accept this one thousand dollars... *(Surprised murmur from everyone. MINNIE feels in her purse.)* It's gone! The money is gone!

(Excited reaction from everyone. The voices die away. There are a

HERR KUTTER, THE BARBARIC BARBER

couple of beats of silence.)

PAT. *(Off SL.) (Calls HANS' real first name)*, it's your line!
HANS. Oh! I haf a suggestion...
BEA. *(Under her breath.)* It's about time!
PAT. *(Off SL.)* That man is going to give me a nervous breakdown! I think he's the reason they invented Valium!
HANS. *(Irritated.)* As I vas saying... Dere's a policeman here, Officer Dan Druff. I suggest he search everyvon before anybody leaves dis room. *(Sotto voice, to HEDDA.)* Back me up!
HEDDA. Oh. Okay. *(She puts her hands on HANS' chest and pushes him backward.)*
HANS. Dat's not vhat I meant!
DAN. *(Stepping forward.)* I'm Dan Druff, and I think Herr Kutter's suggestion is a good one. Ladies, I must ask you to open your purses, and men, empty your pockets.

(Everyone complies.)

HARRY. *(Pulling out the envelope.)* What is this...?
MINNIE. That's it! That's my envelope of money!
DAN. Give me that.

(HARRY gives him the envelope. DAN pulls out the money. Everyone reacts.)

MINNIE. See! Ten one hundred dollar bills! *(Big reaction.)*
HARRY. But I didn't...
LOTTA. *(Cutting in.)* That's why he asked you to dance! So he could steal your money!
HARRY. But...
LOTTA. What a scoop!

HERR KUTTER, THE BARBARIC BARBER

(She writes on her pad furiously, pulling it out of her purse if it's not alreay out.)

    HANS. Do your duty, Officer — arrest dat man!
    LORRIE. Harry...?
    HANS. It's duh klinker for you, kiddo!
    BARBARA. Harry wouldn't steal from anyone!
    SHU. He's innocent!
    DAN. That's for the courts to decide. I'll need to keep this as evidence, Mrs. Bucks. It will be returned to you once the case is closed.
    MINNIE. I understand.
    DAN. *(Taking HARRY's arm.)* Come with me, young man. I'm taking you to the police station.

(They start toward the SR doorway.)

    LORRIE. Oh, Harry...

(She bursts into tears.)

    HANS. *(Crossing to LORRIE.)* You've had an awful shock, my dear. Let us go someplace private vhere I can comfort you. *(He puts an arm around her waist and leads her toward the SL doorway. KITTY and the guests murmur among themselves. Once HANS and LORRIE have passed HEDDA, he turns back and says to her:)* My nefarious scheme vorked perfectly! By stealing duh money from duh old dame's purse und planting it in duh Noggin boy's pocket, I haf succeeded in getting him out of duh vay. Now I can marry Lorrie Ell, ka-knock off her aunt, und inherit millions! *(Everyone freezes and stares at HANS.)* Vhat?

HERR KUTTER, THE BARBARIC BARBER

HEDDA. You dope! You were supposed to say that as an aside to the audience, not to me! Everyone heard you!

HANS. Dey did?

EVERYONE EXCEPT HANS AND HEDDA. You bet we did!

HANS. Uh-oh.

HEDDA. And you treat me like I'm dumb! See what happens when you can't get your part right!?!

DAN. *(Releasing HARRY and starting toward HANS.)* I think you'd better come with me, mister.

HANS. Hold it! *(He tightens his grip around LORRIE's waist and pulls his razor from his pocket with his other hand. He snaps it open. Everyone reacts.)* Don't come any closer!

HARRY. You cad! You...you barbaric barber!

HANS. Yeah, yeah, yeah... Hedda, take duh money from Officer Druff.

(She goes to DAN and takes the money. She will cross back to SR of HANS.)

HEDDA. What are we going to do now, Hans?

HANS. Use dat thousand dollars to get out of here. I don't know about you, but I plan to head back to Germany.

HARRY. Let Lorrie go!

HANS. Not until ve're far avay from here! Den I'll decide vhat I vant to do vid her!

NELL. Dan! Can't you do something to stop him!

DAN. No, Nell — as sloppy as he is with a razor, I don't dare try!

HANS. You had to get in your little dig, didn't you? *(An aside.)* Okay, so tings didn't vork out duh vay I had planned... I knew vhat to do, I just got a little confused. *(To HEDDA.)* See! I do know how to deliver an aside! Come on!

HERR KUTTER, THE BARBARIC BARBER

(He starts to back slowly to the SL doorway, pulling LORRIE. HEDDA follows.)

LORRIE. Harry! Help!
HANS. Duh boy is powerless to rescue you!
HARRY. Oh, no, I'm not! *(He strikes a hammy pose, arms outstretched toward her, and says:)* Oh, Lorrie! I love you more than life itself! Do you love me?
LORRIE. *(Stretching her arms toward him as she's pulled backward.)* Oh, yes, Harry! I love you with all my heart! *(STAGEHAND ENTERS through the doorway SL, holding his triangle. He has removed his coat. For once, he's bold, not afraid of being onstage. With a wicked gleam in his eye, he holds up the triangle right behind HANS, who doesn't see him, and bangs it with all his might. HANS cries out, releases LORRIE, drops the razor, and covers his ears with his hands. LORRIE stamps on HEDDA's foot, causing her to cry out, grabs the money from HEDDA, and runs into HARRY's arms. Big reaction from everyone. DAN crosses to HANS and HEDDA and takes each by the arm.)*
DAN. I'm placing you two under arrest! *(STAGEHAND, with a smug look on his face, does an old-fashioned bow — one arm across the waist, the other across his back — to the audience, then to the other cast members. Everyone applauds. He EXITS SL, very self-satisfied.)* Come with me.

(He leads HANS and HEDDA to the doorway SR.)

LORRIE. You saved me, Harry! You're my hero!
HARRY. True love always finds a way!

(They kiss. The others cheer.)

HERR KUTTER, THE BARBARIC BARBER

HEDDA. Well, if this isn't the pits! You are the worst actor who ever stepped foot on a stage!

HANS. It's the director's fault! We needed more rehearsals! He/She should have helped me with my lines! *(His voice trails off as DAN and they EXIT SR.)* He/She needs to fire that stagehand! If he busted my eardrums, I'll sue...

KITTY. *(Joining HARRY and LORRIE.)* Harry, you were brilliant! If anything had happened to my beloved niece...

HARRY. She's safe, Miss Kitty...and I'll keep her safe always if she will consent to become Mrs. Harry Noggin.

LORRIE. Oh, I do, Harry — I do!

(They kiss again.)

LOTTA. *(After touching the pencil to her tongue and putting the final period to her story:)* The end!

PAT. *(Sticking his head in DL.)* You said it! *(He pops out of sight.)*

CURTAIN

(After the company takes its bows, HANS says to the audience:)

HANS. I just want you to know that all of the comments you heard tonight about my not being able to get my part right were in the script, word for word!

HEDDA. *(Sarcastically.)* Yeah, sure...

(The other actors start to gang up on him, ad-libbing comments like "That's a likely story", etc. HANS backs UC as the others follow, berating him.)

FINAL CURTAIN

HERR KUTTER, THE BARBARIC BARBER

PROPERTY LIST

PRE-SET:
2 hand mirrors - beauty shop cabinet
hair products - beauty shop cabinet
Minnie's purse/coins - beauty shop cabinet
Lotta's purse/coins - beauty shop cabinet
coin bowl - Nell's table

PERSONAL:
mirror on stand - Stagehand
clipboard - Pat
razor strap - Hans & Hedda
razor - Hans
hat - Kitty
clear nail polish - Nell
hair pins - Bea & Boo
invitations - Kitty
invitation - Lorrie
triangle - Stagehand
barber cape - Dan
fake moustache - Dan
coins - Dan
nail brush - Hedda
razor - Pat
mug/shaving lather & brush - Hans
pencil - Hans
towel - Hans
script - Pat
tape on shirt sleeve - Pat
invitation - Harry
mirror frame on stand - Stagehand

HERR KUTTER, THE BARBARIC BARBER

confetti - Stagehand
broom - Stagehand
purse/envelope of money - Minnie
purse/pad & pencil - Lotta
prizes (optional) - Stagehand
potted plant - Hans

HERR KUTTER, THE BARBARIC BARBER

COSTUME PLOT

(All costumes except Pat's and Stagehand's are for the 1900 period)

PAT - jeans or casual pants, modern shirt + tux or suit coat
STAGEHAND - jeans, modern shirt + tux or suit coat
HANS - dark suit, period shirt (pin stripe or pastel with white collar and cuffs), smock; later, tux or suit & bow tie
HEDDA - black everyday dress, smock; later, black gown
KITTY - dress, coat, hat; later, gown
LORRIE - skirt, blouse; later, gown
NELL - skirt, blouse; later, gown
MINNIE - dress; later, gown
LOTTA - dress; later, gown
BOO - dress; later, gown
BEA - dress; later, gown
DAN - policeman's uniform, shirt; later, white tux or suit & bow tie
HARRY - dark slacks, period shirt; later, tux or suit & bow tie
BARBARA - dress; later, gown
SHU - slacks, period shirt; later, tux or suit & bow tie
EXTRAS - men in tuxes or suits & bow ties; women in gowns

(Lorrie and Kitty can have daytime purses when they vist the shops; all the women can have purses going to and at the ball. Minnie and Lotta must have purses in all their scenes.)

Also by

Billy St. John

THE ABDUCTION

THE DISAPPEARANCE OF
THE THREE LITTLE PIGS

HERE COMES THE BRIDE
AND THERE GOES THE GROOM

IS THERE A COMIC IN THE HOUSE?

THE PLOT, LIKE GRAVY, THICKENS

THE REUNION

SENIOR FOLLIES

THE WEREWOLF'S CURSE

YOU COULD DIE LAUGHING

SAMUELFRENCH.COM

BLUE YONDER
Kate Aspengren

Dramatic Comedy / Monolgues and scenes
12f (can be performed with as few as 4 with doubling) / Unit Set

A familiar adage states, "Men may work from sun to sun, but women's work is never done." In Blue Yonder, the audience meets twelve mesmerizing and eccentric women including a flight instructor, a firefighter, a stuntwoman, a woman who donates body parts, an employment counselor, a professional softball player, a surgical nurse professional baseball player, and a daredevil who plays with dynamite among others. Through the monologues, each woman examines her life's work and explores the career that she has found. Or that has found her.

COCKEYED
William Missouri Downs

Comedy / 3m, 1f / Unit Set

Phil, an average nice guy, is madly in love with the beautiful Sophia. The only problem is that she's unaware of his existence. He tries to introduce himself but she looks right through him. When Phil discovers Sophia has a glass eye, he thinks that might be the problem, but soon realizes that she really can't see him. Perhaps he is caught in a philosophical hyperspace or dualistic reality or perhaps beautiful women are just unaware of nice guys. Armed only with a B.A. in philosophy, Phil sets out to prove his existence and win Sophia's heart. This fast moving farce is the winner of the HotCity Theatre's GreenHouse New Play Festival. The St. Louis Post-Dispatch called Cockeyed a clever romantic comedy, Talkin' Broadway called it "hilarious," while Playback Magazine said that it was "fresh and invigorating."

Winner!
of the HotCity Theatre GreenHouse New Play Festival

"Rocking with laughter...hilarious...polished and engaging work draws heavily on the age-old conventions of farce: improbable situations, exaggerated characters, amazing coincidences, absurd misunderstandings, people hiding in closets and barely missing each other as they run in and out of doors...full of comic momentum as Cockeyed hurtles toward its conclusion."
–Talkin' Broadway

SAMUELFRENCH.COM

THE OFFICE PLAYS
Two full length plays by Adam Bock

THE RECEPTIONIST
Comedy / 2m, 2f / Interior

At the start of a typical day in the Northeast Office, Beverly deals effortlessly with ringing phones and her colleague's romantic troubles. But the appearance of a charming rep from the Central Office disrupts the friendly routine. And as the true nature of the company's business becomes apparent, The Receptionist raises disquieting, provocative questions about the consequences of complicity with evil.

"...Mr. Bock's poisoned Post-it note of a play."
– *New York Times*

"Bock's intense initial focus on the routine goes to the heart of *The Receptionist's* pointed, painfully timely allegory... elliptical, provocative play..."
– *Time Out New York*

THE THUGS
Comedy / 2m, 6f / Interior

The Obie Award winning dark comedy about work, thunder and the mysterious things that are happening on the 9th floor of a big law firm. When a group of temps try to discover the secrets that lurk in the hidden crevices of their workplace, they realize they would rather believe in gossip and rumors than face dangerous realities.

"Bock starts you off giggling, but leaves you with a chill."
– *Time Out New York*

"... a delightfully paranoid little nightmare that is both more chillingly realistic and pointedly absurd than anything John Grisham ever dreamed up."
– *New York Times*

SAMUELFRENCH.COM

ANON
Kate Robin

Drama / 2m, 12f / Area

Anon. follows two couples as they cope with sexual addiction. Trip and Allison are young and healthy, but he's more interested in his abnormally large porn collection than in her. While they begin to work through both of their own sexual and relationship hang-ups, Trip's parents are stuck in the roles they've been carving out for years in their dysfunctional marriage. In between scenes with these four characters, 10 different women, members of a support group for those involved with individuals with sex addiction issues, tell their stories in monologues that are alternately funny and harrowing..

In addition to Anon., Robin's play What They Have was also commissioned by South Coast Repertory. Her plays have also been developed at Manhattan Theater Club, Playwrights Horizons, New York Theatre Workshop, The Eugene O'Neill Theater Center's National Playwrights Conference, JAW/West at Portland Center Stage and Ensemble Studio Theatre. Television and film credits include "Six Feet Under" (writer/supervising producer) and "Coming Soon." Robin received the 2003 Princess Grace Statuette for playwriting and is an alumna of New Dramatists.

SAMUELFRENCH.COM

WHITE BUFFALO
Don Zolidis

Drama / 3m, 2f (plus chorus)/ Unit Set

Based on actual events, WHITE BUFFALO tells the story of the miracle birth of a white buffalo calf on a small farm in southern Wisconsin. When Carol Gelling discovers that one of the buffalo on her farm is born white in color, she thinks nothing more of it than a curiosity. Soon, however, she learns that this is the fulfillment of an ancient prophecy believed by the Sioux to bring peace on earth and unity to all mankind. Her little farm is quickly overwhelmed with religious pilgrims, bringing her into contact with a culture and faith that is wholly unfamiliar to her. When a mysterious businessman offers to buy the calf for two million dollars, Carol is thrown into doubt about whether to profit from the religious beliefs of others or to keep true to a spirituality she knows nothing about.

SAMUELFRENCH.COM

www.ingramcontent.com/pod-product-compliance
Lightning Source LLC
Chambersburg PA
CBHW070648300426
44111CB00013B/2321